cover COVER Bible Stud

7 Sessions for Homegroup and Personal Use

Ephesians

Claiming your Inheritance

Trevor J. Partridge

Contents

Introduction

The epistle to the Ephesians gives us the richest exposition of the blessings God has provided for us in Christ. The apostle's mind and heart were full to overflowing with the sense of magnanimous provision made for us by the Father. In fact "in Christ" is a recurring theme in Ephesians, commencing with Paul's salutation in the very first verse, "Paul, an apostle of Christ Jesus by the will of God, To the saints in Ephesus, the faithful *in Christ Jesus*" (my italics).

The small preposition "in", which precedes "Christ", becomes a significant word in the epistle, embracing and encompassing all dimensions of redemption, atonement, justification, sanctification, reconciliation, propitiation, adoption and many other facets of our salvation. Being "in Christ", incorporates the entirety of the eternal work of God in bringing us from death to life through repentance, by way of the cross and Christ's shed blood. To be saved means that we are positionally "in Christ".

It also means that now we are in Christ, there is a magnificent inheritance provided for the saints, enabling us both to be secure in Christ through salvation and to draw on the available power and provision of resurrection life in Christ to work in and through us. It opens up access to a whole new world of spiritual possibility, which the apostle Paul describes as "the incomparable riches of his grace" (2:7), "the unsearchable riches of Christ" (3:8) that, "Having believed, you were marked in him with a seal, the promised Holy Spirit, who is a deposit guaranteeing our inheritance until the redemption of those who are God's possession – to the praise of his glory" (1:13–14). Paul is talking about the wealth of the believer, not in terms of the material prosperity of the world today, focused on personal gain, but in terms of the abundant giving of God's grace. This glorious supply that will reveal even richer and ever-fuller, never-ending splendours from His eternal storehouse. What we know of it already is like the handful of pebbles a child gathers on the seashore that stretches into the vast unexplored depths of the boundless supply of the ocean bed beyond.

It's possible to have an inheritance and never stake your claim to it, either because you didn't know about it or because, although you knew, you just couldn't believe it to be possible and were not bold enough to claim it. Paul assures us the inheritance is there and my prayer is that, through these studies, your awareness of it will grow, that you will take God's Word at face value and be bold enough to make your claim.

With an inheritance, provision is made for someone to be a beneficiary of a legacy or bequest, the recipient of an abundant blessing because of someone else's foresight and provision. The beneficiary can only enter into and enjoy the benefits and blessing of the inheritance after the benefactor dies and the inheritance becomes available. For the inheritance to be passed to the beneficiary, the will of the benefactor needs to be executed and administered by a lawyer, advocate or executor.

Christ has died to secure our salvation and make possible our inheritance. He has returned to the Father and has sent the Holy Spirit who has been given to us to guarantee, make available and administer that inheritance. He is the executor of the divine will. The Greek word used here by Paul is *arrhabon*. It was a word used in business transactions to indicate a down payment, or part payment that secured the full sum. It was a pledge of money or property signifying that the full payment would be made. Paul is telling us here that the Holy Spirit is

God's pledge and guarantee of full provision of the inheritance He has promised to us.

Another recurring and key phrase in this book is "heavenly realms". It speaks of the unseen sphere above the world of sense, substance and material matter, to the spiritual and supernatural dimension. Not something futuristic, a possibility to look forward to some day, but the present active dimension of God's eternal presence and activity, where His blessing and power are freely available. In the third verse, Paul confirms that God "has blessed us in the heavenly realms with every spiritual blessing in Christ". In verse 18, he prays that we might know "the riches of his glorious inheritance in the saints".

Unfortunately, many of God's people live spiritually impoverished lives, having never fully entered into the inheritance that is rightfully theirs. Their lives are spiritually bankrupt and beggared, running just above the empty mark, having allowed the enemy of their soul to rob them of the inheritance that is rightfully theirs. They fail to avail themselves of the daily presence of the Spirit who administers through His gifts and graces the abundant provision of Father God.

Over the next few weeks we will explore some of the things Paul highlights that we can enter into and enjoy as part of our inheritance and also consider what may be holding us back.

WEEK 1

Stop Putting yourself Down

Opening Icebreaker

If you could choose to be an animal, which one would it be, and what are its particular characteristics that you are drawn to?

Bible Readings

- Ephesians 1
- Psalm 139:13–18
- John 15:15–16
- 2 Corinthians 12:9–19

Key Verse: "… he has made us accepted in the Beloved". (Eph. 1:6, NKJV)

Focus: Promise "In Christ" Ephesians 1:6

Opening Our Eyes

The greatest fear of the human heart is rejection. We all long to be accepted and loved, and when we fail to experience that, we hurt badly. Feeling and facing the pain of rejection brings the realisation that there is something in our hearts that no one, even the most loving human being, can fully satisfy. The need for acceptance lies within us at a much deeper level.

Paul opens his letter to the Ephesians, after the salutations of the first couple of verses, by underlining the promise of God's blessings in Christ (v.3). He has set His love and affection upon us, has chosen us (v.4), predestined us (v.5), adopted us (v.5), included us (v.13) and marked us out (v.13) for a place in the royal household of heaven.

There was a time when, in God's sight, we were unacceptable, because of our sin and guilt and shame, but now through forgiveness and salvation we are accepted in Christ. The New King James Version of the Bible puts verse 6 like this "… by which he has made us accepted in the Beloved". What a glorious truth and reality: that we are not just made acceptable, but that we have been accepted in Christ, given the same standing as our Saviour. Even though there are things about yourself you find hard to accept, and things about you that others find hard to accept, stop putting yourself down and believe the promise: You are accepted in the Beloved.

Accepted in the Beloved. What an encouraging and reassuring promise this is. In a world that is constantly searching for approval, acceptance, affirmation and affection, how good to know and savour the reality that through nothing we have done or could do, our standing in Christ is one of full acceptance. We have no need to search any longer for acceptance in the eyes of others or struggle to find it in their nod of approval. God's promised smile is already upon us and He will not love us any more or any less in the future than He does right now.

It is often in moments of failure, in moments of guilt, in times of inadequacy and rejection, that Satan seeks to rob us of this part of our glorious inheritance and standing in Christ. We need to come back to this glorious promise, shake off the impositions others may have put upon us or the false accusations Satan is hurling at us, and stand tall in His presence. If we have sinned we need to understand that, although He rejects the sin, He accepts the sinner who comes to Him with a penitent heart, and through mercy, forgiveness and grace again restores.

In the original Greek text, the word "accepted" is *charitoo (khar-ee-to-o)* and is closely related to the grace word *charis. Charitoo* is defined as "highly favoured", "graced with honour" and "accepted". The only other occasion it is found in the New Testament is when the angel appeared to Mary at the annunciation in Luke 1:28 and said "Greetings, you who are *highly favoured*! The Lord is with you" (my italics). The Lord used this word to tell Mary that she was especially chosen, favoured and selected by Him, for the amazing task of bringing the Christ child into the world. You, too, have been selected and highly favoured for a special task. Believe the promise, accept yourself in Him, enter fully into your inheritance and walk tall. You are accepted in the Beloved.

Discussion Starters

1. Take the word "lavish" in verse 8 and discuss how it is evidenced.

_____

_____

_____

_____

2. Recall an instance when you were affirmed and valued and what effect it had on you.

_____

_____

_____

_____

3. Think of a time when you were rejected and share how it felt.

_____

_____

_____

_____

4. Take the idea of being sealed, in verse 13, and think it through.

_____

_____

_____

_____

5. What are some of the emotional barriers that prevent us experiencing God's acceptance?

_____

_____

_____

_____

6. How can we demonstrate to others the acceptance we feel in God both individually and as a body?

_____

_____

_____

_____

7. Think of an instance of God's goodness that made you feel really accepted.

_____

_____

_____

_____

8. Explore the idea of the potential within us yet to be realised.

_____

_____

_____

_____

9. Talk about ways in which the eyes of our hearts might be enlightened.

_____

_____

_____

_____

10. Tell someone, "I am accepted in the Beloved."

Personal Application

"... that the Father may give you the Spirit of wisdom and revelation." Wisdom is the righteous application of knowledge but it must be accompanied by divine insight **".... that the eyes of your heart may be enlightened."** That our inner vision will enlarge into greater eternal perspective, not head knowledge but a heart experience. **"... in order that you may know him better."** The word "know" incorporates both intimacy and fullness, not knowing about, but knowing that comes from the experience of relationship. **"... the hope to which he has called you."** Hope means assurance and conviction. A certain future. **"... the riches of his glorious inheritance in the saints."** Paul says *in* the saints, not *for* the saints. Deposited in is potential, gifting ability and talent yet to be developed. **"... his incomparably great power for us who believe."** This was the power demonstrated when Christ was raised from the dead. The "power that is at work within us" (Eph. 3:20).

Seeing Jesus in the Scriptures

When Jesus was baptised in the Jordan at the commencement of His ministry, the Father looked down and declared, "This is my Son, whom I love; with him I am well pleased (Matt. 3:17). He repeated it exactly when Jesus was on the Mount of Transfiguration towards the end of His ministry (Matt. 17:5). The AV version says, "This is my beloved Son, in whom I am well pleased." God was so pleased with His beloved Son He declared it to the world. Because you are accepted in the Beloved, He is delighted with you too.

WEEK 2

Please Take your Seat

Opening Icebreaker

Ask the group who has a British passport. Ask what is its significance and why. Can anyone say what is written in the front?

Bible Readings

- Ephesians 2
- Romans 5:12–17
- Ephesians 1:20–23
- 2 Timothy 2:12
- 1 Peter 3:22

Key Verse: "God raised us up with Christ and seated us with him in the heavenly realms in Christ Jesus." (2:6)

Focus: Our Position "In Christ" Ephesians 2:10

Opening Our Eyes

The opening verses of chapter 2 describe the depths from which Christ lifted us, to the heights He has positioned us. Once dead in sin, we are now alive in Christ, and more than alive, seated together with Him in the heavenly realms. Writing to the Romans, Paul said, "... how much more will those who receive God's abundant provision of grace and of the gift of righteousness reign in life through the one man, Jesus Christ" (Rom. 5:17).

Reigning over the devil

In chapter 1, Christ is seated at the right hand of the Father in the heavenly realms far above all, with all things placed under His feet. In chapter 2, Paul declares the incredible fact that we are seated together with Christ. Our inheritance is a seat in the heavenly realms, not in the future but right now. Therefore, what is under His feet also comes under ours. We can walk through this world exercising our position and authority in Christ. There is no need to be pushed around or intimidated by the devil anymore, he is a former resident of heaven, we are current ones. The only power he has over us is when we allow him to rob us of the rightful inheritance of our position.

Reigning over the past

Many people are dogged by their past, conditioned by memories of failure, hurt, rejection and disappointment that drag them down from the heavenly realms. Paul said, "But one thing I do: Forgetting what is behind ..." (Phil. 3:13). You see, the past does not have to dictate and determine our future, keeping us from realising our inheritance in Christ. Release the past, let it go, bring it to the cross, forgive and leave it there. It's as though Paul is saying, "Forget it, move on." That's a decision to bury it at the cross and then step from the cross to the throne room. Take your rightful position, shake off the shackles of the past that have pulled you down, bring your future into focus and receive the inheritance of freedom and joy God has for you now.

Reigning over circumstances

How often have you heard someone reply, when asked how they are doing, "Not bad under the circumstances"? I heard of a businessman who had a sign on his desk that read "Keep looking down". "Shouldn't that say keep looking up?" a Christian friend asked. "No," he said, "I am seated together with Christ and that's to remind me that I don't have to live under the circumstances anymore." When you have the vantage point of a seat at the throne, and a position in the heavenly realms, you can view things from God's point of view. This revolutionises many of the struggles and difficulties we experience, enabling us to respond to His grace, not react to the problem, adding depth and richness to our Christian living.

Reigning in life

This is not something for the future, but the here and now. As we take our position with Him we start reigning in life, one area at a time. Someone has commented, "We can be so heavenly-minded that we are no earthly good." This is not possible, it's only when we are heavenly-minded that we are any earthly good. The whole purpose of our position in Christ is to enable us to draw on His power, living effectively in life, being on time, paying our bills, fulfilling our responsibilities and caring for our families.

Discussion Starters

1. Discuss together Ephesians 1:19b–23; 2:6–7 and Colossians 1:15–20, exploring what our position in Christ means.

2. Taking Ephesians 4:27; James 4:7 and 1 Peter 5:8–9, look at how we should deal with the devil.

3. Looking at John 10:10, how can we be robbed of our inheritance?

4. How did Jesus see life from God's point of view when dealing with the devil (Matt. 4:1–11)?

5. What does putting "childish ways behind me" (1 Cor. 13:11) mean?

6. Explore Philippians 3:13, considering what it means to forget, and its relationship to forgiveness.

_____

_____

_____

_____

7. In what ways can guilt and shame pursue us from the past?

_____

_____

_____

_____

8. Discuss responding to grace rather than reacting to the problem.

_____

_____

_____

_____

9. What are some areas of life we can reign in, by taking control and responsibility?

_____

_____

_____

_____

10. Look at the Personal Application and commit yourself to the everyday walk.

Personal Application

Colossians 1:9 in J.B. Phillips' *Letters to Young Churches* says, "We are asking God that you may see things, as it were, from His point of view by being given spiritual insight and understanding." This is what reigning in life is all about, having God's perspective, and taking control and charge of our lives in the light of it.
Every day:

• Commit your ways to God
• Meditate on truth from God's Word
• Reaffirm your position and standing in Christ
• Remind the devil he is a defeated foe
• Make choices consistent with eternal principles
• Respond to God's supply of grace before reacting to life's circumstances
• Put the past behind you and reach forward to what is ahead

Seeing Jesus in the Scriptures

Jesus Christ built His life on spiritual principles that enabled Him to walk through this world seeing life from God's point of view. He said, "I do nothing on my own but speak just what the Father has taught me. The one who sent me is with me; he has not left me alone, for I always do what pleases him" (John 8:28–29). He recognised He was His Father's child, and therefore that nothing could work successfully against Him. At every crossroad He knew which way to take and was always in the place He should be, seeing the whole meaning of His ministry and purpose on earth – from God's point of view. "... the Son can do nothing by himself; he can do only what he sees his Father doing, because whatever the Father does the Son also does" (John 5:19).

WEEK 3

Keep Dreaming your Dreams

Opening Icebreaker

Write down a dream you have had that has been fulfilled. If you could have a dream for anything, what would it be and why? What dream do you feel God has given you for your life? Do you have a dream that has died?

Bible Readings

- Ephesians 3
- 1 Samuel 17:33–37
- Proverbs 29:18 (AV)
- 1 Corinthians 1:26–31
- 2 Corinthians 9:8
- Hebrews 11

Key Verse: "… to him who is able to do immeasurably more than all we ask or imagine …" (3:20)

Focus: Possibilities "In Christ" Ephesians 3:20

Opening Our Eyes

In chapter 3, Paul says that, though he was less than the least of all God's people, grace was poured upon him in such a way that he was given the privilege and purpose of revealing God's eternal purposes. He prays that we might also experience the deep inner strength of the Spirit, the vastness of God's love, a filling with the fullness of God and a recognition that God can do immeasurably more than we could possibly imagine or think. His grace is upon you, His Spirit will strengthen you, He has a great purpose for your life, His love is immense and the possibilities are enormous, because, "God can do anything, you know – far more than you could ever imagine or guess or request in your wildest dreams!" (Eph. 3:20, *The Message*).

Has God dropped something into your heart that is yet to come into being? Paul here talks about the available resources in God to make things happen, that God's ability to abundantly supply immeasurably more than we can imagine, far exceeds our capacity to receive it. Have you settled for the status quo in life, or do you have aspirations and dreams for the future? Paul here talks about imagining those things that may seem impossible to us at the moment, but are possible in God. Are you dreaming dreams in God? Those dreams and desires begin with a sanctified imagination allowing the Holy Spirit to form an idea, picture or image in our hearts and minds, a creative thought that considers the possibilities of things we want to see happen in our future.

All great inventions and advancements existed first as an idea somewhere in someone's mind. God plants dream seeds within us and can birth a vision in our hearts. Can you believe Him for it? Establishing and pursuing a dream brings focus, perspective, confidence, determination, meaning and energy to our lives. The fulfilment of a dream does not come by sitting back daydreaming, hoping something will happen, but by applying yourself to the task. When Henry Ford set out to create an engine with eight cylinders in one block, his engineers insisted it was an impossibility, but he doggedly stuck to the task. Through trial and error, failure and disappointment, his dream kept him going. One day the breakthrough came, his dream became a reality and the motor car industry was revolutionised.

Realising Your Dreams

- God has a purpose for each of our lives and has deposited dream seeds inside each one of us.

- Don't limit God, take time to let God speak to you about a dream then turn it into a desire.

- Nurture and water your dream seeds in faith and expectancy, making sure the dream is free from personal agenda.

- Deal with memories of failure that hold you back and build on memories of past achievements.

- Choose to own the dream, make it yours, believing not only in the dream but yourself as God's choice.

- Write your dream down with some clear objectives and a plan to move forward to specific goals.

- Be prepared for setbacks, don't give up, decide to pursue it, persistently, diligently and tenaciously.

- When a dream dies, recognise that it is often part of a birth, death and resurrection process.

- Remember, as you obey, so God reveals. God can never take you further than your last act of obedience.

- Don't let others discourage, quash, steal or cause you to give up the dream God has put in your heart.

Discussion Starters

1. Taking Paul's view of himself in verse 8, explore his perspective in 1 Corinthians 1:26–31.

2. What is your definition of a dream?

3. In what ways do we often put ourselves down in relation to our dreams?

4. Discuss what is meant by a sanctified imagination.

5. Identify a memory of failure that prevents you from dreaming a dream.

6. Share some lion and bear stories with each other (see Personal Application).

_____

_____

_____

_____

7. Share together some of the dreams you have and pray together about them.

_____

_____

_____

_____

8. Ephesians 3:20 (AV) says "exceedingly abundantly". Talk through ways in which God's abundance is evidenced.

_____

_____

_____

_____

9. Talk through the points under Realising your Dreams.

_____

_____

_____

_____

Read out loud together as an affirmation, Ephesians 3:20.

Personal Application

The mind has two powerful dynamics, *memory* and *imagination*. Linked together they are very powerful indeed. *Memory* has the ability to inspire or inhibit. Like a video recorder, it captures an image from the past and files it away ready for instant replay. If the memory is painful, negative or of failure, it holds us back. If happy, positive and productive it will inspire and encourage for the future. *Imagination* is a blank canvas or tape, not holding past events, but creating possibilities for the future. Those who achieve great things are able to put behind them unhelpful memories and build on the experiences of the past. When facing Goliath, those around David said it was not possible to slay him, but David had lion and bear stories stored in his memory. He declared that Goliath would suffer the same fate. He linked his memory to a possibility, put his trust in God and his own ability with a sling shot and stones and, as they say, the rest is history (1 Sam. 17:33–37).

Seeing Jesus in the Scriptures

The disciples' dream died at the cross. They had hoped and dreamed that a new kingdom would be established, but it had all appeared to come to a crashing end with the death of Jesus. Hebrews tells us that Jesus saw beyond the cross to the throne. His vision and dream had an eternal perspective that enabled Him to move through the experience of the cross to the eternal presence of His Father and the company of the redeemed. (See Hebrews 12:2.)

WEEK 4

A New Wardrobe

Opening Icebreaker

Exchange your coats and jackets and put them on, otherwise have some different jackets or coats ready, or swap shoes with each other and try them on. They will probably be too baggy or too tight. Discuss how you all felt with clothes or shoes that didn't belong to you and how uncomfortable you felt wearing something that didn't fit you.

Bible Readings

- Ephesians 4
- Joshua 1:1–8
- Romans 12:1–2
- 2 Corinthians 10:1–6
- Philippians 2:11

Key Verse: "… be made new in the attitude of your minds". (4:23)

Focus: Perspective "In Christ" Ephesians 4:22–23

Opening Our Eyes

Paul starts by urging the Ephesians to "live a life worthy of the calling you have received". The call of God is a high and noble calling, and he encourages them to leave their old identity behind and to embrace fully the new calling they have received "in Christ". He sums it up in verses 22–24, when he says *"put off your old self"*, and *"put on the new self"*. Their walk is to reflect their calling.

Paul identifies, in verses 25–32, the unworthy ways we must *put off* as lies, anger, stealing, corrupt conversation, bitterness, rage, slander and malice, basically saying, Look, make a choice, take control, stop doing these things, they are not worthy of your calling. No more lying to cover yourself, no more stealing to get ahead, no more dishonesty to gain advantage, no more gossip to make you feel good, no more anger to get your own way, no more bitterness and self-pity to get attention. Discard your old ways like an old coat or jacket, take them off, get rid of them, don't hold onto them, assign them to the bin. Instead of those old dirty dingy clothes *put on* your inheritance, the robe of righteousness (Isa. 61:10). Like Joseph with his coat of many colours, display the full dazzling colour of God's character – speaking the truth in love, dealing with anger, working in order to give to those in need, speaking words that bless, being kind, compassionate and forgiving.

Paul says, "… be made new in the attitude of your minds" (Eph. 4:23), *put off* the old mindset and *put on* the new mindset, a totally different perspective, from the heavenly realms. (See also Colossians 3:1–3.) The devil robs us of our inheritance, by keeping us wearing the old wardrobe. He clouds our minds, keeping them in ignorance of the liberating truth that sets us free from the old patterns, attitudes and behaviours. Paul urged the Romans, "Do not conform any longer to the pattern of this world, but be transformed by the renewing of your mind" (Rom. 12:2).

How do we renew our minds, in order to live a life worthy of the calling we have received? In writing to the Corinthians, Paul said, "The weapons we fight with are not the weapons of the world. On the contrary, they have divine power to demolish strongholds. We demolish arguments and every pretension that sets itself up against the knowledge of God, and we take captive every thought to make it obedient to Christ" (2 Cor. 10:4–5).

Thinking often becomes so entrenched in our minds that it becomes a "stronghold", a fortress, a castle or a refuge we retreat back to. They are "pretensions" that pose as the normal, the acceptable, setting themselves up as an alternative against the knowledge of the way God wants us to live. We so readily slip back into the old negative and sinful thought patterns, burned into our minds over time through exposure to the ways of the world.

We can choose to take these thoughts captive and submit them in obedience to Christ, "putting them off" through repentance, choosing to embrace the mind of Christ by "putting on" the truth. "Whatever is true, whatever is noble, whatever is right, whatever is pure, whatever is lovely, whatever is admirable – if anything is excellent or praiseworthy – think about such things" (Phil. 4:8).

Discussion Starters

1. From Ephesians 4, make a list of those things that would go under the headings of "Put off" and "Put on".

_____

_____

_____

_____

2. How can thoughts be taken captive? Share your own experiences.

_____

_____

_____

_____

3. Talk through the aspects of "strongholds" and "pretensions" of the mind.

_____

_____

_____

_____

4. Look through the Sermon on the Mount and find the instances where Jesus says, "But I tell you …".

_____

_____

_____

_____

5. Discuss the contrasts between the human reasoning of the day and the divine wisdom of Jesus.

_____

_____

_____

_____

6. Look up the following scriptures: Joshua 1:8; Psalm 1:2–3; 19:14; 63:5–6; 119:9–11; 97–100; Proverbs 4:4. What is biblical meditation and how does it take place?

_____

_____

_____

_____

7. What do you think is the significance of "meditating on your bed", or at night before going to sleep?

_____

_____

_____

_____

8. Talk through the concept that meditation is the digestive system of the soul.

_____

_____

_____

_____

9. Taking the categories of Philippians 4:8, come up with three concrete things for each category.

_____

_____

_____

_____

Personal Application

As we allow our minds to be saturated with God's Word and flooded with truth, the thought patterns built up in them and contrary to Him will be broken up. As we "put off" old thought patterns and discard them, the Holy Spirit rebuilds our thoughts around Christ and His precepts. Renewing our mind is the process of embracing God's Word and turning it into spiritual faith and energy, where biblical principles are turned into working realities. Allowing it to turn around in our thinking over and over again until we begin to talk to ourselves about it, allowing it to penetrate, permeate and saturate our thinking. Our minds are cleansed from wrong thought patterns "by the washing with water through the word" (Eph. 5:26).

Seeing Jesus in the Scriptures

The Sermon on the Mount, beginning in Matthew chapter 5, has been called Christ's manifesto for kingdom living. It is, in fact, the revealed mind of Christ, the heavenly perspective. He taught in complete contrast to the mindset of the day. The phrase constantly repeated after Jesus has stated the perception of the day is, "But I tell you", followed by eternal truths from the heart of heaven. "You have heard that it was said, 'Love your neighbour and hate your enemy.' But I tell you: Love your enemies and pray for those who persecute you" (Matt. 5:43–44). He exhorted them to *put off* their old thinking, embrace the truth and *put on* a new mindset. "Let this mind be in you, which was also in Christ Jesus" (Phil. 2:5, AV).

WEEK 5

A Time for Everything

Opening Icebreaker

Give a time chart to each member of the group and fill in how you use your time on a typical week. When completed, get into threes to share your findings and any implications you may discover.

Bible Readings

- Ephesians 5
- Ecclesiastes 2:17–26; 3:1–14
- Mark 6:31
- 2 Corinthians 6
- Colossians 4:5

Key Verse: "Make the best use of your time, despite all the evils of these days. Don't be vague, but grasp firmly what you know to be the will of the Lord." (Eph. 5:16–17, J.B. Phillips)

Focus: Priorities "In Christ" Ephesians 5:15–16

Opening Our Eyes

Have you ever wished for a 36-hour day? Surely it would relieve the pressure and resolve the issue of not enough hours in the day to get everything done. Our lives are so often full of frenetic activity, leaving a trail of unfinished tasks. Paul, in writing to the Ephesians (v.16), addresses the issue of time as a sacred trust given to us by God to use and invest wisely and conscientiously.

"Make best use of your time"

There are numerous books and courses on time-management, but actually time is impossible to manage. It is constant, 60 seconds a minute, 60 minutes an hour and 24 hours a day. Paul doesn't say "Manage your time", but "Make best use of it". The issue is not time-management, but management of ourselves in relation to the time we have. You can't manage time, but you can manage yourself.

"Despite all the evils of these days"

One of the evils of the day is the continuous treadmill of activity. Almost everyone you talk to seems stressed in some way or other. Stress not only comes from the pressures, demands and general pace of modern-day life, but research shows that ineffectiveness also comes from tension within. Many demands are made on us which, although urgent, may not be important. All too often we major in minors and minor in majors, letting the urgent things distract us from the important, the good things from the best. We need to put first things first, omit lesser things and determine God's priorities in our lives. One of the devil's strategies is to rob us of our time through endless activity.

"Don't be vague"

Procrastination is the thief of all time. Don't be vague,
be decisive. God has given us time to be our servant,
unfortunately it has made us its slave, pushing us around
from one thing to the next. Start by taking stock and
evaluating just how your time is being spent. Unless we
stop and sort out the multiplicity of tasks, we will always
be running ourselves ragged, doing a lot but accomp-
lishing little. When we stop to evaluate, it's clear the
problem is not a shortage of time but a need to
re-evaluate priorities. Re-evaluate your use of time in the
light of eternal values and plan your activities to achieve
maximum effectiveness with minimum weariness. When
God told man to rest on the seventh day, it was also to
enable him to re-evaluate his priorities, looking back over
the past week and forward planning the coming one.
Make a time each week on your "day of rest", somewhere between the activities of a busy Sunday church
programme, for re-evaluation. If you don't take control
of your life, it will be controlled by the demands and
pressure of others.

"Grasp firmly what you know to be the will of the Lord"

Take control of your life, establish your priorities in the
light of eternal values. Reserve a few moments each day
to prayerfully take stock of your life and follow the
Sabbath principle. Delegate tasks to others, don't be a
people-pleaser, and learn to say no. Don't give in to
constant demands from others. Refuse to be controlled
by continual deadlines. Find out what resources are
available and make use of them. Don't get saddled with
an unreasonable workload, or over-commit yourself,
beyond your capacity. Take time off for rest and
relaxation, fun and enjoyment.

Discussion Starters

1. What are some of the things that can motivate us to become over-committed?

_____

_____

_____

_____

2. Why do some of us find it hard to involve others or delegate?

_____

_____

_____

_____

3. What are some of the dynamics and internal tensions that might drive people who are workaholics?

_____

_____

_____

_____

4. What does the Bible have to say about slothfulness and laziness (Prov. 6:6–11; Rom. 12:11)?

_____

_____

_____

_____

5. How did Jesus prepare Himself to deal with the demands of a busy day (Mark 1:35–39)?

_____

_____

_____

_____

6. How did His eternal perspective help Jesus deal with pressures and demands put on Him (John 11:1–6)?

_____

_____

_____

_____

7. Work through the points under "Grasp firmly what you know to be the will of the Lord".

_____

_____

_____

_____

8. What steps can be taken to overcome the pattern of disorganisation?

_____

_____

_____

_____

9. How do we stop being a slave of time and make it our servant? How does this relate to eternity?

_____

_____

_____

_____

10. Look up the points and references under the section Seeing Jesus in the Scriptures.

Personal Application

"Do not get drunk on wine, which leads to debauchery. Instead, be filled with the Spirit" (v.18). A drunk man loses all track of time, is totally disorganised, disorientated, out of control and slothful. Paul says don't be like this, instead be filled with the Spirit. You see part of being filled with the Spirit has to do with how we handle ourselves in relation to the time God has given us stewardship over. If we will make the effort to take a grip of this area of our lives the Holy Spirit will guide, direct and empower us to lead fruitful, productive and stress-free lives.

Seeing Jesus in the Scriptures

Jesus Christ accomplished more in three short years than we do in a lifetime. It was not the amount of time He had which was significant, but what He did with it. He had an eternal perspective (John 9:4). He had a clear sense of purpose and mission (John 10:10). He was a hard worker (Mark 1:21–35). He had the right priorities (Mark 1:35). He did not give in to the demands of others (John 11:3–6). He delegated to others (Mark 3:14–15). He did not let turbulent circumstances steal His sleep (Mark 4:37–38). He was not distracted from the task (John 7:3–9). He finished the work His Father gave Him to do (John 17:4). He was able to declare triumphantly on the cross not, I am finished, but "It is finished". He had completed the work His Father sent Him to do (John 19:30).

WEEK 6

Energised for Life

Opening Icebreaker

Write down what comes into your mind when you think of the word "energise" and what you connect to it. Discuss this.

Bible Readings

- Ephesians 5:15–20
- Acts 8:9–24
- Romans 8:1–11
- 1 Corinthians 12:1–11
- Galatians 5:16–26

Key Verse: "Instead, be filled with the Spirit." (5:18)

Focus: Power "In Christ" Ephesians 5:17–18

Opening Our Eyes

We saw earlier in Ephesians that, when we are saved, we are sealed with the Holy Spirit, as a mark of God's ownership. But, more than that, the Holy Spirit is the deposit, or down payment, guaranteeing our inheritance, the executor of the divine will here on earth (Rom. 8:16).

Paul gives the command here, "Be filled with the Spirit", not as an optional extra, but as an absolute requirement. The verb used here in the Greek is the present continuous tense, and better translated as "Be being filled". It is not a once-only or one-off specific spiritual experience, either during or after conversion, but an ongoing release of the Spirit's work, energising, empowering and enabling our lives; the regular inflow of His presence and power, leading to an overflowing and outworking of His gifts and graces available as part of every believer's inheritance. This is a command, because there are so many things that force their way into our lives demanding our attention, that it is possible to allow the Spirit's work to become marginal and peripheral, rather than central.

Walk in the Spirit (Gal. 5:16–21, AV). Paul says that if we "walk in the Spirit", we will "not fulfil the lust of the flesh". The deeds of the flesh come easily to us, we don't need to be taught them, they are part of the package Adam left us. One of the works of the Holy Spirit is to bring conviction of righteousness and sin to our lives (John 16:8). If we are continually filled with the Spirit, when deeds of the flesh seek to assert themselves, the siren of God's conviction sounds in our spirits. As we respond, we will be empowered to walk in the ways of the Spirit.

The fruit of the Spirit (Gal. 5:22–25). Paul says that not
only are we able to walk righteously, by not pursuing the
deeds of the flesh, but that the Spirit produces fruit in our
lives. We cannot strive to be fruitful, we do the cultivating
and He produces the fruit within us. When we are filled
with the Spirit, walking in His ways, preparing the soil,
the fruit of the Spirit is the natural outworking of growth.
It is the work of the indwelling Spirit that enables us to
live in a godly way, displaying the character of Christ.

The witness of the Spirit (Acts 1:8). Jesus promised His
disciples that when He returned to His Father in heaven
He would send the gift of the Holy Spirit to empower
them from on high, and that as a result they would be
effective witnesses for Him. To be filled with the Spirit
emboldens us to testify freely and openly witness to the
goodness of our God; making "the righteous … as bold
as a lion" (Prov. 28:1).

The demonstration of the Spirit (1 Cor. 12:1–11).
The Holy Spirit makes available to us His gifts that are
administered by Him through us in order to move us
from the natural realm of functioning to the supernatural
dimension of miracles, signs and wonders.

Worship in the Spirit (Eph. 5:19–20). As we are
continually filled with the Spirit, walking in the Spirit,
evidencing the fruit of the Spirit, giving Spirit-empowered
witness, demonstrating the supernatural work of the Spirit,
the consequence will be that we will share together in
psalms, hymns and spiritual songs, singing and making
melody in our hearts and giving thanks.

Discussion Starters

1. Discuss the analogy Paul makes between drunkenness and being filled with the Spirit.

_____

_____

_____

_____

2. In Acts 1, look at the observers' comments and the impact of the Holy Spirit on Peter.

_____

_____

_____

_____

3. Taking Galatians 5:16–21, look at the deeds of the flesh and identify some ways we easily slip into them.

_____

_____

_____

_____

4. Talk through being convicted or convinced of righteousness as being different from convicted of sin.

_____

_____

_____

_____

5. Suggest practical ways the fruit of the Spirit listed in Galatians 5:22 is manifested in our lives.

_____

_____

_____

_____

6. Discuss why Paul said "fruit of the Spirit" and not fruits of the Spirit.

_____

_____

_____

_____

7. When was the last time you shared your faith with someone else?

_____

_____

_____

_____

8. Have you received any of the ministry gifts of the Holy Spirit?

_____

_____

_____

_____

9. Do you feel you need a fresh infilling of the Holy Spirit?

_____

_____

_____

_____

Spend some moments in worship together, allowing the Holy Spirit to make melody in your hearts.

Personal Application

People hold different views about being filled with the Spirit. Some say it takes place at conversion, others say it is a separate and subsequent experience, accompanied by speaking in tongues or other manifestations and expressions. Jesus said, "… you will receive power when the Holy Spirit comes on you" (Acts 1:8). There is no question that when the promised Holy Sprit fell on the disciples, significant things happened and extraordinary expressions were witnessed, so much so that onlookers asked, "Are these people drunk?" Whatever your view, you need to be full of the Holy Spirit. Be open to Him to move as He chooses, recognising He is symbolised as both a dove and a fire. Allow Him to fill you to overflowing. Remember, it's not how high you can jump, but whether you can walk straight when your feet touch the ground.

Seeing Jesus in the Scriptures

When John was baptising in the Jordan, he declared that Jesus would baptise with the Holy Spirit and with fire (Matt. 3:11). When Jesus was baptised by John, the Spirit of God descended on Him like a dove (Matt 3:16). Jesus declared, "Whoever believes in me, as the Scripture has said, streams of living water will flow from within him. By this he meant the Spirit, whom those who believed in him were later to receive" (John 7:38–39). He also said, "If you then, though you are evil, know how to give good gifts to your children, how much more will your Father in heaven give the Holy Spirit to those who ask him" (Luke 11:13).

WEEK 7

Dressed for Success

Opening Icebreaker

Get the group to write on a piece of paper their response to the statement: "Christians have more trouble in their lives after they become Christians than before." Get into two groups, with those who agree in one group and those who disagree in another group, listing their reasons. Share the lists and have a general discussion on the findings.

Bible Readings

- Ephesians 6
- Romans 8:35–37; 13:12
- 2 Corinthians 10:4
- Hebrews 4:12
- 1 Peter 5:8–9

Key Verse: "Put on the full armour of God ..."
Ephesians 6:11

Focus: Protection "In Christ" (Ephesians 6:13)

Opening Our Eyes

In chapter 4, Paul exhorts, "nor give place to the devil" (v.27, NKJV). The word place in Greek is *topos* giving us the word topography, being territory, region and ground. The enemy's strategy is to take ground and territory from us, exploiting our weaknesses, catching us off guard and robbing us of our rightful inheritance. The apostle says, don't surrender, don't give ground to him.

He returns to this theme and says, "Be strong in the Lord and in his mighty power." How? By putting on "the full armour of God so that you can take your stand against the devil's schemes" (Eph. 6:11). Don't be pushed around or intimidated by your adversary. Stand, and having done all, continue to stand. Stand against evil, stand for what is right. To effectively stand against the wiles of the devil we must put on the whole armour of God, not as a defence to hide behind, but as protection to march forward without fear, to reclaim the devil's territory. Of course we will be attacked as we advance forward, but with every piece of the armour in place, nothing can stop, destroy or defeat us. The six pieces of armour we need to put on for protection are:

The belt of truth to protect against the devil's lies and deception. The devil's primary weapon is to lie. He used this against Adam and Eve to great advantage, and he has been using it ever since as his major strategy. This piece of armour holds all the others in place.

The breastplate of righteousness to protect against the devil's accusations and taunts. We are in "right standing" with God through the redemptive, atoning work of Christ on the cross who alone makes us worthy. Satan hates to be reminded that he was defeated at the cross.

The shoes of peace to protect against confusion and division, "For God is not a God of disorder but of peace" (1 Cor. 14:33). We know the devil sows confusion wherever he goes causing division at every opportunity. With the shoes of peace on we can walk through confusion.

The shield of faith to protect against discouragement and fear. The devil might hurl his best flaming arrows at us, but with the shield of faith in position we have a guard to protect us with no possibility of them penetrating, hurting or harming us.

The helmet of salvation to protect against doubt and unbelief. The assurance of salvation brings the confidence "that he who began a good work in you will carry it on to completion" (Phil. 1:6), and that He is "the author and finisher of our faith" (Heb. 12:2, AV).

The sword of the Spirit which is the Word of God. This is the only weapon listed for offensive attack, it is quick and powerful, sharper than a two-edged sword. Paul uses the Greek word *rhema* here, signifying the spoken word. A weapon is only useful if it is used, and we can defeat the adversary of our soul by speaking the Word of God as Christ did on the mount of temptation by saying to the devil, "It is written ..." (Matt. 4:7–10)

It's time to start marching, to move from the comfort zone to the combat zone, out of the pew and into the trenches. Let's kit up, put on our battledress, take the battle to the enemy, regain the territory and see the kingdom of light overcoming the kingdom of darkness.

Discussion Starters

1. What does "Don't give place to the devil" mean?

_____

_____

_____

_____

2. Define what might be a territory? Are some territories more significant than others?

_____

_____

_____

_____

3. What does it mean to take a stand on something?

_____

_____

_____

_____

4. List the kind of issues we need to stand up for and stand firm on.

_____

_____

_____

_____

5. In what ways does the devil seek to disrupt our peace with God and with others?

_____

_____

_____

_____

6. What does it mean to be more than a conqueror?

_____
_____
_____
_____

7. What are territories or areas that we can reclaim?

_____
_____
_____
_____

8. Work through the pieces of armour and explore them further.

_____
_____
_____
_____

9. What do you think the apostle Paul meant when he exhorted us to pray with all kinds of prayer?

_____
_____
_____
_____

10. Discuss what it means to put on the armour of God.

_____
_____
_____
_____

Personal Application

Prayer is our lifeline, the oxygen supply enabling us to replenish our spiritual energy levels for battle. It only takes a couple of victories in battle to become self-sufficient and complacent. David threw the stone, but he cried, "The battle is the Lord's" (1 Sam. 17:47). Prayer keeps us in that place of constant dependency on Him. Sometimes in battle, we don't quite know how to pray, or what for. We can call on the Spirit of God to help. (See Romans 8:26.) After putting on the armour, Paul exhorts us to " pray in the Spirit on all occasions with all kinds of prayers and requests" (Eph. 6:18).

Seeing Jesus in the Scriptures

Jesus said of the devil, "He was a murderer from the beginning, not holding to the truth, for there is no truth in him. When he lies, he speaks his native language, for he is a liar and the father of lies" (John 8:44). When Jesus came declaring, "I am the truth," His powerful ministry precipitated a violent outburst of demonic activity, and part of His ministry was going directly into the devil's territory to reclaim it (Matt. 4:24; 8;16,28,33; 9:32; 12:22; Mark 7:25; 9:25). He declared, "the prince of this world is coming. He has no hold on me"(John 14:30). He commissioned His disciples to drive out the devil (Matt. 10:1–8; Mark 3:14–15; 6:12–13; 16:15–17). Probably the most significant thing about His ministry was not the miracles, these were seen throughout the Old Testament, but that He took authority over the devil, casting out demons.

Leader's Notes

Week 1: Stop Putting yourself Down

Icebreaker

Very often when this exercise is done with a group, people will select animals that are cuddly and accepted and loved as pets and family friends. Some, though, may select wild animals. Gently draw out why they have selected the ones they have, finishing with those who selected cuddly ones, exploring if maybe it was because they were loved and accepted as part of the family that they chose them. Draw out the fact that there is a longing in all of us to be accepted.

Aim of the Session

The objective of looking at the first chapter in the book of Ephesians is to underline that we have an inheritance that very often we are not accessing and utilising because we do not feel worthy or accepted. To expose the group to the wonderful truths Paul records, get someone to re-read to the group verses 1–14 with excitement and enthusiasm and get members of the group to give their response and reaction. These verses were in fact one sentence, and if the passage can be read that way, you will catch something of how it came tumbling out of the apostle Paul. Using Discussion Starter 1, explore the idea of God's lavishness as expressed through these first 14 verses. Open up the concepts of chosen, adopted, included, predestined, marked out – pointing out that these are all active initiatives from God to us. Focusing on verse 6, use Discussion Starters 2–7 to open up discussion on the subject of acceptance and rejection, being willing to share something out of your own experience of an occasion of rejection. The goal here is to affirm group members, helping them to see that God accepts us, not on the basis of what we do or do not do, but because of who we are.

We don't need to try to be like anyone else: God doesn't need more of the same, it's our uniqueness that draws Him to us. Always remember you are God's choice. Drawing from the Seeing Jesus in the Scriptures section, emphasise our positioning in Christ through the forgiveness of sin.

Taking it on from verse 15, look at the things that Paul prays that we might know, and explore with the group in what ways we can come to know them better. How can we develop our relationship of intimacy with Him? Daily devotions, time spent in the Word, entering into acts of worship, participating in active fellowship, times of quiet reflection and solitude. Explore the concept of calling and see if any of the group has a strong sense of calling. Couple that with the idea of hope being a knowable assurance, an inner conviction of the heart. Think through together what potential talents, gifts and abilities may be lying dormant in each one. Ask members of the group what gifts and abilities they see in each other. This might be a good time to spend praying this issue through together. Take Romans 8:11 and explore the idea of God's power at work in our mortal bodies. The word power here being to energise, or to give energy to.

Closing Exercise
Using the last Discussion Starter, break into twos and say to each other, "I am accepted in the Beloved," with the other person responding with the affirmation, "And I accept you too." Get them to declare it a second time with conviction and passion. Then declare it out together as a group.

Week 2: Please Take your Seat

Icebreaker

Bring your passport to the group and hold it up when getting a response to the questions. Explain that our passport is our right by birth and part of our national inheritance. Read the statement inside and ask what it means. If we are citizens of the United Kingdom, for example, it puts us in the position of standing in the name of Her Majesty and having her government backing to pass without let or hindrance.

Aim of the Session

Paul underlines our condition without Christ: dead (v.1), disobedient (v.2), debauched (v.3) and doomed (v.3). Explore these four areas briefly, reminding the group where they have come from in life. That we have now been made alive in Christ, saved by grace (vv.4–5), but more than that, we have not only been pulled out of the pit, but given a position and access in the heavenly realms alongside Christ who is seated at the right hand of the Father. Using Discussion Starter 1, underline the death, resurrection and ascension of Jesus, the positioning of Christ in heaven, and what our position seated with Him means. The aim of the session is to help us to recognise our position in Christ and, rather than be ruled by life, to take our rightful authority by reigning in four particular areas:

1. Over the devil. All things are placed under Christ's feet, including the devil. He was defeated once and for all at the cross. We are now seated with Christ in heavenly realms, therefore the devil is under our feet, too. He has no place or part in heaven, Jesus said, "I saw Satan fall like lightning from heaven" (Luke 10:18). Using Discussion Starter 2, look at how we can use the authority vested in us to deal with the devil. Encourage each other to:

- Re-affirm your position in Christ (Eph. 2:6)
- Remind the devil he is a defeated foe through Christ's shed blood (Rev. 12:10–11)
- Identify any attacks, submit yourself to God and resist them (James 4:7)
- Refer the devil to what God has said in His Word (Matt. 4:4–10)
- Rejoice in your position, the devil is under your feet (Luke 10:20)

2. Over the past. Using Discussion Starter 5, explore the verse referred to. The thing that militates against the development and flow of love in our lives is so often the inner child of the past, easily hurt, demanding, self-centred, holding grudges, settling scores, jockeying for position etc. The past retains a hold on us, influencing and affecting the present and threatening the future. Paul talks about doing "one thing". Using Discussion Starter 6, help the group to think through whether they need to make a move in their position by forgiving and forgetting what others may have done and, using Discussion Starter 7, to forgive themselves and move on, from being a victim of the past to being a victor in the future.

3. Over circumstances. Using Discussion Starter 8, consider the concept of looking "down" on our circumstances and responding to God's corresponding supply of grace, rather than reacting to the problem. The important lesson here is learning to take our perspective from the position of the throne, by asking God to enable us to see life from His point of view, bringing out that God's point of view and heaven's perspective is found first in His Word, and that grace is provided through Christ's resurrection power.

4. In life. Using Discussion Starter 9, talk about the practical areas of life where we can take control and responsibility and Discussion Starter 10 to set a daily pattern of reigning in life.

Week 3: Keep Dreaming your Dreams

Icebreaker

Use the icebreaker as a way of opening up the subject of pursuing a dream. Break the group down into threes to discuss their dreams and aspirations. There may be some who have non-identifiable dreams who will need encouragement to think the issue through. There may be others whose dreams have died and you will need to be sensitive to them.

Aim of the Session

To see that in Christ there are possibilities and potential yet untapped. That God has infinite resources to accomplish great things, and that it is the limitation of our own small thinking that so often prevents significant achievements from taking place.

Cover the first six verses of the chapter, drawing out the special purpose Paul had of revealing to the Ephesians the mystery of Christ, pointing out that a mystery in Scripture is not something that cannot be understood, but something that is revealed by the Spirit of God to His apostles and prophets (vv.4–5).

Using Discussion Starter 1, explore verses 7–9 and how Paul viewed himself, coupling it with his comments to the Corinthians in the first chapter, focusing on the foolish, the weak, the lowly and the despised, and drawing out what God is able to do with such people and how he viewed God's grace as the key. Look also at 2 Corinthians 12:7–10.

Look at Paul's prayer (Eph. 3:14–19) – the dimensions

of God's love and the key word fullness in verse 19. The Greek word here is *plerom*. When the ancients conducted a census in a city, if every dwelling place in it was fully occupied it was listed as *pleroma*. When the crew of a ship was at full strength, it was listed as *pleroma*, indicating a full complement. It was also used to describe a cargo net when it was crammed full, or the hollow places in the hold which had been filled to maximum capacity. Paul's prayer was that they would be full to capacity with God's supply of abundance – not just to be filled with God, but to be filled with the fullness of God.

This brings us to verse 20 and God's ability to do exceedingly abundantly above all that we can ask or think. Take the first paragraph of Opening Our Eyes to summarise what Paul is saying. Using *The Message* translation of Ephesians 3:20, introduce the idea of dreaming dreams and draw out from the Icebreaker and Discussion Starter 2 the definition of a dream in this context and what holds us back from dreaming. Bring out that past failures or hurts prevent us from dreaming again because we don't want to experience failure again, or feel further pain or humiliation. Using such examples as Moses, David, Peter and Thomas, point out that God is the God of the second chance. The goal is to get people thinking through the fact that God has made available abundant resources in Christ, to do amazing feats for Him. These will not happen unless we sow some dream seeds of doing exploits for Him.

Take the ten points under Realising Your Dreams and talk them through one at a time, laying a foundation for a time of prayer. Pray for those who have no sense of vision or dream, for those whose dreams have stalled or died. Draw out here that God often births a vision, allows it to die so that we take our hands off it and then resurrects it in His power and strength. Pray for those who are in the process of seeing their dreams come into being.

Week 4: A New Wardrobe

Icebreaker

The objective here is to bring out how uncomfortable we feel wearing other people's clothes or shoes, and yet we settle so often for wearing the old garments that the Bible describes as filthy rags.

Aim of the Session

To consider Paul's admonition to *put off* the old self and *put on* the new self, by recognising old patterns of thinking we may not have discarded, and embracing new patterns of thought revealed in God's Word. Using the first Discussion Starter, look at the contrasts Paul highlights, and, using the kind of illustrations in paragraph two of Opening Our Eyes, identify some life patterns that go with them. Moving on to Discussion Starter 2, begin to explore the idea of taking thoughts captive, drawing out the point that when someone is taken captive it is usually with an amount of effort or force. Taking captive carries the idea of active pursuit not compliant surrender.

Point out that old thought patterns can become strongholds or fixed positions in our minds. Often described as misbeliefs, or deceptions, the Bible calls them pretensions, because they parade themselves as the truth or plausible facts. They often become the bedrock of our belief and value systems, because they have come out of our experience, training or parentage and we have come to accept them as fact. Statements like, "I am a failure", "Self-discipline is hard to achieve", "I must please everybody", "My childhood will always affect me" etc. become self-talk statements, embedded in our thought processes and need to be examined in the light of truth.

Taking the thought expressed in the section Seeing Jesus in the Scriptures, divide the group into threes giving different portions of the Sermon on the Mount to them, to look through the instances where Jesus says, "But I tell you ...", getting them to share what they find in relation to the expressed wisdom of the day and the divine wisdom of Jesus.

Using Discussion Starter 6, apportion the scriptures to the smaller groups asking each group to come up with what the Bible says about meditating on God's Word, and what is promised to those who will take the time to do this. Focus particularly on Joshua 1, and the great challenge that faced him, and also the analogy in Psalm 1:2–3. Meditation in the original language meant to roll a word, thought or phrase around in your mind, to continually contemplate, ponder or dwell on it. To view it from every angle in your imagination, weighing it and studying it carefully in your mind. To do this over and over again until you begin to talk to yourself about it, allowing it to penetrate, permeate and saturate your thinking, "communing with your soul". The process is like the cow chewing the cud, swallowing it, bringing it up again, chewing it over, repeating this a number of times until it is fully digested and gestated. The significance of meditating before going to sleep is that the last thoughts in our mind lie in our subconscious as we sleep, and the best thoughts are God's. That is why the psalmist said, "I ... meditate on thee in the night watches" (Psa. 63:6, AV).

Sum up by sharing that so often we are robbed of our full inheritance by being held in an old mindset. We can put it off, by recognising it as a pretension, taking it captive to Christ and turning away from it as we are renewed in the attitude of our minds by putting on the truth through meditating on God's Word.

Week 5: A Time for Everything

Icebreaker

The purpose is to get the group thinking about and looking at how you all organise and use your time. I suggest you draw up a simple time chart of seven columns, one for each day of the week with 24 spaces in each column for each hour of the day, one for each person. Take about 10 minutes to fill them in, then get into threes to share what you are discovering. There will probably be one of two responses, either people can't fit everything in, or they discover gaps they didn't realise were there. Not everyone will find it easy, but encourage people to stick with it, but don't put pressure on anyone who may feel uncomfortable doing it.

Aim of the Session

To help people realise that they can take control of their lives and time in the light of eternity. That one of the riches of our inheritance is to be able to invest our time and make an impact in eternity.

Using the time chart from the Icebreaker exercise, explore with Discussion Starters 1 and 2, the issue of over-commitment, and some reasons why this might be, such as a need to feel wanted, the need to please others, the need to feel significant, the need for acceptance etc. In other words, it's often to meet some need in us. It's not that we can't delegate to others, although that's often the excuse, but that we won't, because we feel threatened they may do it better than us, or we'll feel less important. Consider the issue of what drives people to become workaholics and look at things such as the need to prove ourselves, financial gain, status, climbing the promotional ladder etc. Go on to talk about the fact that there may be big gaps in the time chart we can't really account for, or long periods watching television. Come back to the

Ephesians picture of a drunken man and draw out the points in the Personal Application, exploring the issue of slothfulness and laziness.

Two different words are used in the New Testament for time, *Chronos* (Acts 1:7; Gal. 4:4) from which we get chronology. A period of duration, measurable time, the order of events that includes the calendar, the decade, the century, the four seasons. In the light of eternity, we have responsibility to order our lives in relation to it. *Kairos* (2 Cor. 6:2; Gal. 6:9–10; Col. 4:5–6) means the immediate moment, the here and now, the moment of opportunity that passes, it can be missed and never retrieved. It is gone with no guarantee we will have the opportunity again. It is special and specific and we need to seize the moment. Bring out the point that we have a responsibility to so order our live in the *chronos* that God has the opportunity to bring us *kairos* opportunities that we are not too busy or stressed to seize. In 1 Chronicles 12:32 we read the men of Issachar had understanding of the times so knew what Israel ought to do. They were sensitive to the moment of opportunity and devised a wise plan of action. Lead the group through the four points of the verse, commenting and expanding on them, finishing with the seven things to consider in taking control of our lives in order to grasp more firmly the will of the Lord. Encourage them not to let the devil rob them of their inheritance in this area and the eternal accolade "Well done, thou good and faithful servant … enter thou into the joy of thy lord" (Matt. 25:21, AV).

Week 6: Energised for Life

Icebreaker

The objective is to emphasise that energy is dynamic, a power source that gives momentum and movement, vibrancy and life. That God has a supply of divine energy flowing from the turbines of heaven. If the production of human, natural and mechanical energy can make such an impact on us how much more will supernatural energy, delivered by the Holy Spirit (Rom. 8:11).

Aim of the Session

To explore what it means to be filled with the Spirit and encourage the group to open themselves to a fresh infilling. Using Discussion Starter 1, draw out that Paul is warning them not to get drunk because it debilitates and disorientates, whereas the Holy Spirit energises and invigorates. He is not saying, Don't get drunk on wine, instead get intoxicated with the Spirit. The observers on the Day of Pentecost suggested this, because they were astonished and could find no other explanation, but Peter got up and lucidly, with great oratory, preached on the resurrection with around 3,000 people getting saved. That's what being filled with the Spirit can do. Using Discussion Starter 2 and comparing it to Matthew 26:69–75, look at the difference it made immediately in Peter's life.

Using Discussion Starter 3, break into groups of three, dividing the 15 things listed in Galatians 5 amongst them, asking them to consider how we might easily slip into them. For example, sexual immorality: taking the words of Jesus, we see that this can be done in the heart (Matt. 5:27–28) the internet, page three girls, TV programmes, movies etc – not suggesting that this would be deliberate, but easy to slip into. Use Discussion Starter 4 to talk about that, as we allow the Holy Spirit to fill us, there becomes a heightened awareness of what is unrighteous. By responding to the Spirit's promptings He provides us with power to turn away, walking in the paths of righteousness. When He fills us we become far more sensitive to what is unrighteous.

Using Discussion Starter 5, open up the whole area of the fruit of the Spirit being evidenced in our lives. Get everyone to come up with practical outworkings. For example, self-control is not speeding, not comfort-eating, not being sarcastic etc. This is not achieved through superhuman effort, but by a work of the fullness of the Spirit in our lives, and if these things are a continual struggle to us, it is a sure sign that we need a fresh infilling of the Holy Spirit. Use the sixth one to draw out that these things listed are not isolated and disparate, but are all fruit from the same tree and come as a group. Some suggest that love is the fruit and everything that follows is an expression and outworking of it. Have you ever seen a young couple madly in love? What do they exude? Joy. Explore the rest of the fruit of the Spirit in this way with the group.

Gently draw out from the group if they are experiencing the impact of the Spirit's empowering in their lives for witness, ministry and worship, using positive testimonies in the group to encourage, not to make others feel guilty but hungry for more of the things of the Spirit. Pray together and seek the Lord for a fresh infilling. Start this time with some worship songs, inviting the Holy Spirit to come and do a fresh work among you and fill each of you to overflowing.

Week 7: Dressed for Success

Icebreaker

Break into two groups, taking opposite points of view, or otherwise play devil's advocate. There will be good argument for both views, such as, "When we lived for the devil, he was on our side." "Then how do you account for the troubles the unsaved continue to experience?" On the other hand, someone might say, "When we got saved surely we received the joy of the Lord along with many other blessings, so our troubles must be less." "Yes, but now the devil is against us we are attacked more, think of poor old Job." The reality is, it is neither more or less, in that the sun shines on the righteous and the unrighteous alike, cancer and road accidents have no preference for either Christians or non-Christians. The issue is not the fact that trouble comes our way, but that God has made provision to enable us to deal with life. For our protection, for example, we have the armour of God.

Aim of the Session

To recognise that, as part of our inheritance, God has provided His armour to protect and equip us against the attacks of the devil. We don't have to live life in defeat and fear, we need only to take advantage of the protection provided. We have inherited a wardrobe, or a "war" "robe" to fit us for the task, that comes straight from the heavenly armoury.

Explore together what it means to hand over territory in our lives to the devil, and what some of the strategic areas of territory might be. You are looking to establish those that the armour will combat: lies and deceptions, accusations and taunts, confusion and division, discouragement and fear, doubt and unbelief. Using Discussion Starters, underline our need to be resolute in standing firm, pointing out that the devil exploits timid, wobbly

Christians, seizing territory they have gained, and bringing them back into bondage. Talk about some of the issues we need to stand *for* and those we need to stand *against*.

In response to Discussion Starter 6, referring to Romans 8:35–37, bring out that to be more than a conqueror means to win the battle with consummate ease and little effort expended. If a boxer wins after 15 hard rounds, he is the winner. If he were to win the same fight with the first punch in the first second of the first minute, he would be more than a conqueror. Work through the six pieces of armour expanding on each one.

When you have covered the armour, point out that this is not an analogy or an illustration, we are soldiers in a battle, this is for real and it is our battledress. Paul tells us to put it on, and we need to do that actively. Pray, then encourage the group in an attitude of prayer to put on the armour. Have your Bibles close to hand. We talked about the creative sanctified imagination a couple of weeks ago, now here's an opportunity to use it. With eyes closed, get everyone to imagine themselves in front of the mirror, getting dressed as they normally would in the morning, only on this occasion they are going to put on their battledress, the armour of God. Take them through each piece, one at a time, describing it, commenting on it and putting it in position. When it comes to the sword of the Spirit get them to pick up their Bibles. Then spend some further time in prayer, allowing the Holy Spirit to move through the prayers. Send each other out ready for active service.

National Distributors

UK: (and countries not listed below)
CWR, Waverley Abbey House, Waverley Lane, Farnham, Surrey GU9 8EP.
Tel: (01252) 784710 Outside UK (44) 1252 784710

AUSTRALIA: CMC Australasia, PO Box 519, Belmont, Victoria 3216.
Tel: (03) 5241 3288

CANADA: CMC Distribution Ltd, PO Box 7000, Niagara on the Lake, Ontario L0S 1JO.
Tel: 1800 325 1297

GHANA: Challenge Enterprises of Ghana, PO Box 5723, Accra.
Tel: (021) 222437/223249 Fax: (021) 226227

HONG KONG: Cross Communications Ltd, 1/F, 562A Nathan Road, Kowloon.
Tel: 2780 1188 Fax: 2770 6229

INDIA: Crystal Communications, 10-3-18/4/1, East Marredpally, Secunderabad – 500 026.
Tel/Fax: (040) 7732801

KENYA: Keswick Bookshop, PO Box 10242, Nairobi.
Tel: (02) 331692/226047 Fax: (02) 728557

MALAYSIA: Salvation Book Centre (M) Sdn Bhd, 23 Jalan SS 2/64,
47300 Petaling Jaya, Selangor.
Tel: (03) 78766411/78766797 Fax: (03) 78757066/78756360

NEW ZEALAND: CMC Australasia, PO Box 36015, Lower Hutt.
Tel: 0800 449 408 Fax: 0800 449 049

NIGERIA: FBFM, Helen Baugh House, 96 St Finbarr's College Road, Akoka, Lagos.
Tel: (01) 7747429/4700218/825775/827264

PHILIPPINES: OMF Literature Inc, 776 Boni Avenue, Mandaluyong City.
Tel: (02) 531 2183 Fax: (02) 531 1960

REPUBLIC OF IRELAND: Scripture Union, 40 Talbot Street, Dublin 1.
Tel: (01) 8363764

SINGAPORE: Armour Publishing Pte Ltd, Block 203A Henderson Road,
11–06 Henderson Industrial Park, Singapore 159546.
Tel: 276 9976 Fax: 276 7564

SOUTH AFRICA: Struik Christian Books, 80 MacKenzie Street,
PO Box 1144, Cape Town 8000.
Tel: (021) 462 4360 Fax: (021) 461 3612

SRI LANKA: Christombu Books, 27 Hospital Street, Colombo 1.
Tel: (01) 433142/328909

TANZANIA: CLC Christian Book Centre, PO Box 1384, Mkwepu Street, Dar es Salaam.
Tel/Fax: (022) 2119439

USA: CMC Distribution, PO Box 644, Lewiston, New York, 14092-0644.
Tel: 1800 325 1297

ZIMBABWE: Word of Life Books, Shop 4, Memorial Building,
35 S Machel Avenue, Harare.
Tel: (04) 781305 Fax: (04) 774739

For email addresses, visit the CWR website: www.cwr.org.uk

Cover to Cover
Bible Study Guides

These exciting new study guides from the *Cover to Cover* range have been created to provide a unique resource for group and individual study sessions lasting between one and two hours.

The seven stimulating sessions in each title include opening icebreakers, Bible references, discussion starters and suggestions for personal application. There is an introduction that sets the topic in context as well as helpful notes for group leaders.

The Image of God
His Attributes and Character
ISBN: 1-85345-228-9

The Tabernacle
Entering into God's Presence
ISBN: 1-85345-230-0

The Uniqueness of our Faith
What makes Christianity Distinctive?
ISBN: 1-85345-232-7

Ruth
Loving Kindness in Action
ISBN: 1-85345-231-9

Mark
Life as it is Meant to be Lived
ISBN: 1-85345-233-5

Ephesians
Claiming your Inheritance
ISBN: 1-85345-229-7

£3.49 each